# Lenten Resources
For Worship Leaders

*An Anthology*

CSS Publishing Company, Inc., Lima, Ohio

LENTEN RESOURCES FOR WORSHIP LEADERS

Copyright © 1997 by
CSS Publishing Company, Inc.
Lima, Ohio

The original purchaser may photocopy material in this publication for use as it was intended (i.e. worship material for worship use; educational material for classroom use; dramatic material for staging or production). No additional permission is required from the publisher for such copying by the original purchaser only. Inquiries should be addressed to: Permissions, CSS Publishing Company, Inc., P.O. Box 4503, Lima, Ohio 45802-4503.

Scripture quotations are from the *Good News Bible,* in today's English Version. Copyright © American Bible Society 1966, 1971, 1976. Used by permission.

Scripture quotations are from the *New American Standard Bible,* © 1960, 1962, 1963, 1968, 1971, 1972, 1973, 1975, 1977 by The Lockman Foundation. Used by permission.

Scripture quotations are from the *Revised Standard Version of the Bible,* copyrighted 1946, 1952 ©, 1971, 1973, by the Division of Christian Education of the National Council of the Churches of Christ in the USA. Used by permission.

**Library of Congress Cataloging-in-Publication Data**

Lenten resources for worship leaders : an anthology / Alexander H. Wales ... [et al.].
    p.   cm.
Includes bibliographical references.
ISBN 0-7880-0716-5 (pbk.)
    1. Lent—Prayer-books and devotions—English. 2. Liturgies I. Wales, Alexander H., 1948-
BV85.L43   1997
263'.92—dc20                                                  96-38676
                                                                                                   CIP

This book is available in the following formats, listed by ISBN:
    0-7880-0716-5   Book
    0-7880-0886-2   Mac
    0-7880-0887-0   IBM 3 1/2
    0-7880-0888-9   Sermon Prep

PRINTED IN U.S.A.

*Let us praise God
for the gift of his Son
who became the light of the world.*

# Table of Contents

1 — The Service Of Diminishing Lights     9
    A Worship Ceremony For Sundays In Lent
    by Alexander H. Wales

2 — Resources For The Lenten Season     21
    Litanies And Meditations
    by Kathryn W. Orso

3 — Justified By Greed     43
    Monologue Of A Pharisee
    For Lent Or Good Friday
    by Lynda Pujadó

4 — The Passover — Haggadah     51
    A Traditional Seder Service
    by Robert L. Linder and Rabbi Sol Oster

5 — A Good Friday Vigil     77
    Service Of Scripture And Meditation
    by Alexander H. Wales

6 — Shadows Around The Cross     81
    A Tenebrae
    by Ralph Dessem

# *1*

# The Service Of Diminishing Lights

### A Worship Ceremony For Sundays In Lent

### *by*
### Alexander H. Wales

## Author's Preface

Here's something that might be useful in making your congregation's preparation for Lent more meaningful. The Service of Diminishing Lights can be used at the beginning or end of a worship service to put an emphasis on the weeks that rapidly move from Ash Wednesday to Easter Sunday morning. Like the Advent Wreath, the circle of gathering darkness created by the candles and the crown of thorns serves as a constant reminder of the role of human sin in bringing about the crucifixion and the need for Resurrection.

By participating in a weekly rite as a part of the worship experience, individuals can use the silent time available surrounding this service to contemplate their role in the Lenten story. Families, individuals, young and old can be used as participants in this service, as well as acolytes, church officers, and other worship leaders.

My thanks to the Worship Committee of First Presbyterian Church, Warrensburg, for suggesting the development of such a service and its involvement in creating the setting for the Good Friday service as well.

May your Lenten season lead you to an empty tomb, a chorus of Hallelujahs, and a summer of ...

Peace,

Alexander H. Wales

# How To Use The Service

**The Preparation**

To use the material included in this service you will need:

**A crown of thorns** — created from a handicrafts person in your church or purchased from a variety of sources, including flea markets and craft shows.

**Seven candles and holders** — these may fit within or around the crown of thorns or may even be a seven-tiered candelabra. Candle color is at your discretion. Perhaps that box of assorted leftover Advent candles might be used, or white tapers would be just as suitable. One large candle, the Christ Candle, should be designated to be the last candle extinguished. We have traditionally used the white candle from our Advent wreath.

**A candle extinguisher** — either a snuffer that many homes have for general use or an acolyte staff. Blowing out a candle at the appropriate moment may not seem as worshipful, unless done with great care and dignity.

Candles should be lighted before or at the beginning of the worship service. When originally used, this service occurred just prior to the benediction at the conclusion of worship. Each week, the candle extinguished the week prior was covered and not lighted again, though it remained in the crown of thorns as a reminder of the passing weeks of Lent. This service could also be used at the beginning of worship to set a more somber, contemplative tone, or during a time of offering as a meditative setting for the giving and receiving of gifts.

On Good Friday, the crown of thorns with the Christ Candle in the center of the crown becomes the focal point of the worship experience. All candles except the Christ Candle are removed. As the service concludes, the Christ Candle is extinguished and the worshipers are left in total darkness for prayer and contemplation.

**Using The Service Of Diminishing Lights**

As noted above, the service may be placed at any time during a worship experience, although it may fit better at the beginning or end of worship. The printed material that follows is blocked so that more than one participant may be involved each week. Participants may read one block, the entire page, or several paragraphs, depending upon the manner you choose to use.

# Ceremony For The First Sunday Of Lent

During Lent, we remember the events that led Jesus to his crucifixion. He had come into the world to bring hope and light, but at every turn there were those who sought to extinguish that light. He offered healing and wisdom, yet his gifts were often rejected by those filled with hatred and fear.

We read in the fourth chapter of the Gospel of Luke: Jesus went to his hometown, Nazareth, and on the Sabbath, he went as usual to the synagogue. He stood up to read the Scriptures and was handed the book of the prophet Isaiah. He unrolled the scroll and read, "The Spirit of the Lord is upon me, because he has chosen me to bring good news to the poor. He has sent me to proclaim liberty to the captives and recovery of sight to the blind, to set free the oppressed and announce that the time has come when the Lord will save his people."

Jesus rolled up the scroll and gave it back to the attendant and sat down. All the people in the synagogue had their eyes fixed upon him, as he said to them, "This passage of scripture has come true today, as you heard it being read."

When the people in the synagogue heard this, they were filled with anger. They rose up, dragged Jesus out of town and took him to the top of the hill on which their town was built. They meant to throw him over the cliff, but he walked through the middle of the crowd and went on his way.

Jesus had said, "A prophet is never welcomed in his hometown." A little of the light which had come into the world was snuffed out by the people who watched Jesus grow up.

*(Extinguish one of the candles in the circle of the crown of thorns.)*

# Ceremony For The Second Sunday Of Lent

During Lent, we remember the events that led up to the crucifixion. Jesus had come to bring hope and light to the world, but at every step there were those who willingly tried to put out that light. He brought grace and forgiveness, but these gifts were often rejected by those filled with hatred and fear.

We read in the Gospel of Matthew in the twelfth chapter: It was the Sabbath, and Jesus went to a synagogue, where there was a man with a paralyzed hand. Some people were there who wanted to accuse Jesus of doing wrong, so they asked him, "Is it against our law to heal on the Sabbath?"

Jesus answered, "What if one of you has a sheep and it falls into a deep hole on the Sabbath? Will you not take hold of it and lift it out? And a man is worth so much more than a sheep! So then, our Law does allow us to help someone on the Sabbath." Then Jesus said to the man with the paralyzed hand, "Stretch out your hand."

The man stretched out his hand, and it became well again, just like the other one. Then the Pharisees left and made plans to kill Jesus.

Even when Jesus was healing, there were those who could not accept the power and mercy of God. As the Pharisees left to make plans to kill Jesus for healing on the Sabbath, a little of the light which had come into the world was snuffed out by people Jesus had come to save.

*(Extinguish one of the remaining candles in the crown of thorns.)*

# Ceremony For The Third Sunday Of Lent

During Lent, we remember the events that led up to the crucifixion. Jesus had come to bring hope and light to the world, but at every step there were those who could not accept the power of that light. He brought grace and forgiveness, but these gifts were often rejected by those filled with great love for other things.

We read in the Gospel of Mark: As Jesus was going on his way, a man ran up, knelt before him and asked, "Good teacher, what must I do to receive eternal life?"

"Why do you call me good?" Jesus asked him. "No one is good except God alone. You know the commandments: do not commit murder; do not commit adultery; do not steal; do not accuse anyone falsely; do not cheat; respect your father and mother."

"Teacher," said the man, "ever since I was young, I have obeyed all these commandments."

Jesus looked straight at the man with love and said, "You need only one thing more. Go and sell all you have and give the money to the poor, and you will have riches in heaven; then, come and follow me."

When the man heard this, gloom spread over his face, and he went away sad, because he was very rich.

When Jesus spoke the truth, there were those who could not face its light, and they turned away. Every time one of these turned away, a little of the light that had come into the world was put out.

*(Extinguish one of the remaining candles in the crown of thorns.)*

# Ceremony For The Fourth Sunday Of Lent

During Lent, we remember the events that led up to the crucifixion. Jesus had come to bring hope and light to the world, but at every step there were those who could not accept the power of the light. He came to meet the people's needs, but there were those who misunderstood the kind of needs that Jesus meant to fill. Because he would not do what they wanted, they rejected him.

According to John, Jesus was teaching a large crowd who had followed him because they had seen his miracles of healing the sick. Jesus saw the large crowd of more than 5,000 men, and asked Philip, "Where can we buy enough food to feed all these people?"

Philip knew that they didn't have enough money to buy even a small amount for everyone. But Andrew, Simon Peter's brother, said, "There is a small boy who has five loaves of barley bread and two fish, but they will certainly not be enough to feed all these people."

Jesus had the people sit, and then took the bread, gave thanks to God, and distributed it to the people. He did the same with the fish. Everyone had as much as they wanted, and when the disciples gathered what was left, they filled twelve baskets with the pieces of the barley loaves.

Seeing this miracle that Jesus had performed, the people there said, "Surely this is the Prophet who was to come into the world!" Jesus could sense that they were about to make him king by force, so he went off again to the hills to be by himself.

Jesus came into the world to change it, not to be made to fit into some mold that others felt was right. When Jesus refused to be what others wanted, they turned their backs on him, and a little of the light that had come into the world was put out.

*(Extinguish one of the remaining candles in the crown of thorns.)*

# Ceremony For The Fifth Sunday Of Lent

During Lent, we remember the events that led up to the crucifixion. Jesus had come into the world to bring hope and light, but at every step there were those who could not accept the power of that light. He came to create a new relationship between God and human beings, but there were those who had other ideas. Because he could not be manipulated, they sought to kill him.

In the Gospel of Matthew we read: When Jesus had finished teaching, he said to his disciples, "In two days, as you know, it will be the Passover Festival, and the Son of Man will be handed over to be crucified."

The chief priests and the elders met together in the palace of Caiaphas, the High Priest, and made plans to arrest Jesus secretly and put him to death. "We must not do it during the festival," they said, "or the people will riot."

Then one of the twelve disciples — the one named Judas Iscariot — went to the chief priests and asked, "What will you give me if I betray Jesus to you?" They counted out thirty silver coins and gave them to him. From then on, Judas was looking for a good chance to hand Jesus over to them.

Betrayed by a kiss from a friend for thirty pieces of silver ... anyone could have been the one. Jesus came as the truth, but it was too brilliant for those who liked the darkness. As the small bag of coins was traded from hand to hand, a little of the light that had come into the world went out.

*(Extinguish one of the remaining candles in the crown of thorns.)*

# Ceremony For The Sixth Sunday Of Lent

During Lent, we remember the events that led up to the crucifixion. Jesus had come to bring hope and light to the world, but at every step there were those who struggled with the consequences of that light. He came as a friend of sinners and many knew him, but even those who were close to him would often fail to be faithful. When he would depend on them the most, they rejected him.

When Jesus and the disciples were at supper in the upper room, a discussion arose among the disciples about who was the most faithful disciple. Peter claimed that esteemed honor. But Jesus told them that the cup from which he was about to drink was too bitter for any of them to accept. One by one, each would forsake him.

Peter said, "I will not forsake you, Lord. I will follow you to the ends of the earth and suffer what you suffer." Jesus replied to him, "Yes, Peter, you will suffer what I suffer and more, but before the cock crows this morning, three times will you betray me."

After Jesus was arrested, Peter followed the crowd and warmed himself by a fire while Jesus was being questioned. As he sat there, a serving maid from the house saw him and said, "Aren't you one of his disciples?" Peter said, "No, I am not." Another heard him answer and said, "You are a Galilean. Surely you are one of his followers." Again Peter said that he did not know Jesus. A little while later, still another man came up to the fire and said, "Didn't I see you with this Jesus when he was teaching?" With anger in his voice, Peter said, "I told you. I never knew this man!" In the distance, a cock crowed. Peter glanced up and saw Jesus looking at him through the doorway. Peter turned away and ran from the courtyard, with tears streaming down his cheeks.

Even those who loved him most were unable to support him in his darkest hour. When they could have been there, they went into hiding, allowing Jesus to suffer and die alone. And as his friends abandoned him into the hands of his enemies, a little of the light that had come into the world went out.

*(Extinguish the remaining candle in the crown of thorns.)*

# 2

# Resources For The Lenten Season

### Litanies And Meditations

### by
### Kathryn W. Orso

Reprinted from *As We Love And Forgive: Resources For The Lenten Season*, published by CSS Publishing Company, Lima, Ohio.

## Litany For Forgiveness

Pastor: We have sinned in many ways.
People: Forgive us, Lord.

Pastor: We are filled with anger and hatred.
People: We hurt each other needlessly.

All: Forgive us, Lord.

Pastor: We are filled with jealously and envy.
People: We resent it when others have more than we.
All: Forgive us, Lord.

Pastor: We are afraid and lonely.
People: We don't take risks, even for Your sake.
All: Forgive us, Lord.

Pastor: We are selfish and proud.
People: We feel better than others, and are insensitive to their needs.
All: Forgive us, Lord.

Pastor: We are lazy and apathetic.
People: We ignore the needs of others. We don't know they exist.
All: Forgive us, Lord.
For these and all our sins, forgive us, Lord.

Amen.

# Litany for Palm Sunday

Pastor: This is the day the Lord has made.

**People: Hosanna to the King!**

Pastor: This is the day Christ rode into Jerusalem.

**People: Hosanna to the King!**

Pastor: He was King and was hailed as royalty.

**People: Hosanna to the King!**

Pastor: We praise him as our King and Lord.

**People: Hosanna to the King!**

Pastor: We glorify his holy name.

**People: Hosanna to the King!**

Pastor: We magnify his mighty acts.

**People: Hosanna to the King!**

**All:** **We praise and glorify him,
Now and forever more. Amen.**

# Litany For Easter

Pastor: Christ is risen!
**People: He is risen indeed!**

Pastor: Christ has overcome the power of death.
**People: He is risen indeed!**

Pastor: We are filled with the hope of eternal life.
**People: He is risen indeed!**

Pastor: We are filled with the love his resurrection assures.
**People: He is risen indeed!**

Pastor: We are filled with the faith that eternal life will be ours.
**People: He is risen indeed!**

Pastor: We are filled with the knowledge of complete forgiveness.
**People: He is risen indeed!**

Pastor: He died that we might live.
**People: He is risen!**

**All:** **Christ is risen. Hallelujah!**

# Meditation: Forgiveness Is Peace

Peace is hard
  To achieve.
Peace is hard
  To understand.

Peace is the absence of conflict.
  But it's so much more.
Peace is the smile on a face.
  But it's so much more.
Peace is the holding of hands.
  But it's so much more.

Peace is
  Quiet and tranquil.
    But so much more.
Peace is
  Active and dynamic.
    But so much more.

All around us
  There is hurt.
  There is hunger.
  There is abuse.

And peace seems
  So remote.
  So elusive.

In our world
  Tensions are rampant.
  Arms races continue.
  People starve.
And there is no peace.

Bombs are falling.
People are being killed.
Governments are quarreling.
    Will there ever be peace?

In our country
    Power plays prevail.
    Racial struggles are evident.
    Many are hungry.
And there is no peace.

The rich get richer.
The poor get poorer.
The weak get weaker.
    Will there ever be peace?

In our communities
    Street fights occur.
    Murders take place.
    Neighbors hate.
And there is no peace.

Tenements flourish.
Taxes rise.
Graft continues.
    Will there ever be peace?

In our families
    Arguments over little things,
    Disagreements over big things,
    Not speaking about many things.
And there is no peace.

Husbands swearing.
Wives nagging.
Children screaming.
    Will there ever be peace?

In our churches
    We don't like the sermons.
    We can't stand the music.
    We won't support the program.
And there is no peace.

Councilmen are furious.
Ministers are critical.
Lay people are angry.
    Will there ever be peace?

High-sounding hymns
    We sing loudly.
Soul-searching prayers
    We offer sincerely.
But there is no peace.

Juvenile courts.
Divorce courts.
Criminal courts.
    Mistreated children.
    Disagreeable parents.
    Flagrant lawbreakers.
Will there ever be peace?

We work for peace
    To raise money.
    To find homes.
    To fight hunger.

We write letters for peace
    To our president.
    To our congressmen.
    To our newspapers.

We pay for peace
> Through our taxes
>> To the government.
> Through our tithes
>> To the church.

We pray for peace
> For wisdom.
> For patience.
> For hope.

And there is no real peace.
Will there ever be peace?

There'll be no peace
With individuals
> Who save face
>> By hurting others,
> Who prove themselves
>> By denying others.

There'll be no peace
In neighborhoods
> Who value property
>> More than people,
> Who prize possessions
>> More than compassion.

There'll be no peace
Through leaders
> More concerned with history
>> Than with honesty.
> More aware of status
>> Than of justice.

There'll be no peace
Through nations
    More serving of self
        Than respecting of others
    More sure of themselves
        Than accepting of others.

We long for world peace.
We long for personal peace.
    We pray.
    We work.
    We pay.
Painfully.
Arduously.

World peace
    How can there be?
    When there's so little
Personal peace?

Early Christians had
    Trials
    Tribulations
    Troubles.
But they found peace
Somehow, somewhere.

Hated by the Jews,
Scorned by the Greeks,
Persecuted by the Romans,
    They found peace
    Somehow, somewhere.

In the early church, too,
    There was fighting.
    There was jealousy.
    There was division.
But some found peace.
Somehow, somewhere.

There were Jews.
There were Gentiles.
  Brothers in Christ,
  Different in tradition,
Who found peace.
Somehow, somewhere.

To build peace,
We must find peace.

To find peace,
We must find forgiveness.
  For peace is forgiveness,
  And forgiveness is peace.

Personal peace means
Personal forgiveness
  Beginning with us.
    Not feeling guilty
      When tired and discouraged
    Not feeling shame
      When lonesome and disappointed.

We're human.
We're real.
  We feel bad
  Some of the time.
    We make mistakes
    Part of the time.
      We are sinful
      All of the time.
And it's hard to find peace.

Personal peace requires
Personal forgiveness.
  Accepting our humanity,
  Recognizing our mistakes,
  Admitting our sinfulness.
And we'll find peace.

Starting today
Forgiving yesterday
Looking ahead
    There is peace.

We are free
    From our past
    From our punishment
    From our problems
We free ourselves,
As we forgive ourselves.
    And we find peace.

Doors are open.
Power is received.
Potential is expanded.
    In creative growth,
    In positive action,
We find peace.

Peace is forgiveness.
Forgiveness is peace.

Peace is
Forgiveness of others:
    Their unkept promises
    Their unkind remarks
    Their uncontrolled tempers.
    We hate.
    We belittle.
    We dislike.
And we find no peace.

Big things
Little things
    Often excusable
    Sometimes not excusable
But always forgivable,
If we really want peace.

We needle and nag
We probe and question
And we find no peace.

We forgive and forget
We love and accept
And we find peace.

Listening, not judging,
   Our youth
   Our minorities
   Our oppressed
   Our lawbreakers
And in listening
We find peace.

Hearing, not criticizing,
   Our families
   Our friends
   Our neighbors
   Our leaders
And in hearing
We find peace.

In our listening,
In our hearing,
   We lose
      Indifference
      Hatred.
   We express
      Concern
      Forgiveness.
And we find peace.

Peace is forgiveness.
Forgiveness is peace.

God's forgiveness
    No judgment
    No criticism
    No punishment
Just complete forgiveness.
And we have peace.

God's acceptance
    Of our evil thoughts
    Of our malicious lies
    Of our hateful acts
Just complete acceptance.
And we have peace.

God's love
    Through all our sins
    Through all our shortcomings
    Through all our bitterness
Just complete love
And we have peace.

God's forgiveness.
God's acceptance.
God's love.
    Peace, perfect peace.

Peace is forgiveness.
Forgiveness is peace.

Lord, make us builders of peace
    In our families
    In our neighborhoods
    In our country
    In our world.
        As we forgive ourselves,
        As we forgive others,
        As we receive God's forgiveness,
We become builders of peace.

## Meditation: You Make The Difference

You make the difference
It's all up to you.

Whether you love
Whether you hate
    Whether you will
    Whether you won't
It's all up to you.

In your loving
In your doing
In your being
    You make the difference.

For being
And doing
And loving
    Apart from you
    Are nothing.

The greatest thing
In the world
    Is that
    Really
        You do make the difference.

God has given you freedom.
Complete freedom.

He doesn't force you
To love him or
To receive his love.
    He doesn't make you
    Accept his forgiveness
        Or to be forgiving of others.

He doesn't coerce you
To worship him or
To sing his praises.
    It's all up to you.

You're free.
    To love
    To forgive
    To worship
        Or not to love
        Not to forgive
        Not to worship.

God's love
Sets us free.
    Free to choose
        To live in heaven or in hell
        To live today or
            To wait until tomorrow.

In Jesus' story
About the prodigal son,
    The Father freed his son,
    with no strings attached.

        He didn't set limits.
        He didn't tell his son
            What to do or not to do.
        He didn't tell his son
            Where to go or not to go.

He gave him freedom.
    The boy chose himself
    What to do and where to go.
The boy himself made the difference.

In Jesus' life
He set his disciples free,
    With no strings attached.

He didn't set limits
   For his followers
He didn't tell his friends
   Not to deny him
   Not to desert him
   Not to betray him.
He gave them freedom.

God just will not violate
Our freedom.
   He will not dictate our choices.
   He will not control our lives.

You have to make the choice.
   You have the right
   You have the privilege
      To follow him or to desert him
      To choose his way or to deny him
      To obey his commands or to disobey him.

You yourself make the difference.

And the beauty is
God still loves you.
   No matter what you decide
   No matter if you reject him
      Or if you forsake him
God still loves you.

   Jesus loves me, this I know
   For the Bible tells me so.
      Jesus loves me when I'm good
      When I do the things I should.
      Jesus loves me when I'm bad
      Though it makes him very sad.
   Yes, Jesus loves me!

God loves you
No matter what
    So it is up to you.
You decide
You choose
    You make the difference.

God's love
Is not dependent
    On your acceptance of it.
But your acceptance of
God's love
    Makes the difference.

By giving you freedom
    To choose
    To decide
God gives you the chance
    To develop
    To grow
To be a person
    Of dignity
    Of worth.

    Knowing God's love
Feeling loved and respected
    You will draw
    On hidden powers.
        You will discover
        Inner resources.
You will feel the difference.

God doesn't lock us in
God doesn't box us in.
    God frees us
        With the opportunity
        To make mistakes
            With the freedom
            To experiment.

You are free.
> You don't have to be afraid
> Of failure.
>> You don't have to fear
>> Criticism.

God loves you!

God has shown you the way.
God has granted you forgiveness.
God has surrounded you with love.
> Your acceptance
> Or your rejection
>> Makes the difference.

It's all up to you!

# Litany Of Confession

Leader: We come before you, God, knowing we have broken your laws.
Group: **We are very sorry, God.**
Leader: There is so much in life we give a higher priority than your will. Money, work, play. Sports, leisure, fun. Almost everything for ourselves and our family comes first.
Group: **We are very sorry, God.**
Leader: We carelessly use your holy name. We thoughtlessly neglect to pray and to worship you.
Group: **We are very sorry, God.**
Leader: We often begrudgingly go to church. Or we don't go at all when we know we should.
Group: **We are very sorry, God.**
Leader: We give many excuses for not respecting our parents. We blame them, rather than feeling guilty ourselves.
Group: **We are very sorry, God.**
Leader: In the name of justice or of world peace, we forget the sanctity of life. We take life from other human beings, created by you. We are often filled with hatred that kills the spirit of people whom you love.
Group: **We are very sorry, God.**
Leader: We tell "dirty" jokes and laugh at off-color stories. We think impure thoughts and sometimes have immoral desires.
Group: **We are very sorry, God.**
Leader: We often misuse our God-given talents. We fail to deal honestly with all men, in our desire to get more for ourselves.
Group: **We are very sorry, God.**
Leader: We sometimes say less than the whole truth. Or we hurt someone by maliciously telling the truth. Our words, the true and the untrue, are said carelessly, and without love.

**Group:** **We are very sorry, God.**
**Leader:** We forget our blessings, wishing we had what our friends have. We envy each other. We are jealous of one another.
**Group:** **We are very sorry, God.**
**Leader:** We know your laws, although it really doesn't seem that we do. We have not obeyed them. Sometimes willfully. Often carelessly.
**All:** **We are truly sorry. Forgive us, we pray. Amen.**

## Litany For Peace

Pastor: O Lord, help us to love our neighbors.
**People: We want to live in peace.**

Pastor: Help us to love ourselves, dear Lord.
**People: We want to be at peace.**

Pastor: Help us to love you, our Lord and God.
**People: We want to feel your peace.**

Pastor: Help us love with all our heart;
**People: Help us love with all our soul;**
Pastor: Help us love with all our strength;
**People: Help us love with all our mind.**

All: So we will have your peace.

# 3

## Justified By Greed

Monologue Of A Pharisee
For Lent Or Good Friday

*by*
**Lynda Pujadó**

# Justified By Greed

*A Biography of a Pharisee*

**AT RISE:** *(A Pharisee boldly comes on stage and discusses his adamant position against the person of Jesus Christ. The crucifixion, which he helped to instigate, has occurred. The resurrection has not.)*

Let me tell you, I wasn't pleased at all about this carpenter's son called Jesus doing the things he was doing. It was wrong. We Pharisees have our rules and regulations concerning every facet of life. We have hundreds of rules so we can remain pure and I know them all because I am a devoted and blameless Pharisee. Undoubtedly, I am better than other people and I am glad for it. I hope you understand how important it is to be a religious Pharisee. I can't impress you enough with my importance and prestige. Being a Pharisee is a total way of life, a business for ourselves even. You know, I'm sure, how important it is to have a good job.

When Jesus started doing these certain magic signs which people call miracles, and discussing the Scriptures, we Pharisees became angry. It wasn't his place to do any of the things he was doing. It wasn't his place to know and understand the holy words, either. He debated the interpretation of Scripture in our synagogues with undue authority. We became rightfully angry. We are the highest form of authority there is and he did not recognize our importance. He often degraded our level of status. This was all wrong from any standpoint. He was only the son of a poor peasant woman from Nazareth, and Nazareth itself is an obscure village with no importance whatsoever.

Not only was his source of power in doing signs questionable, but he was taking large numbers of the population away from being dedicated and affectionate to us. This would affect our future jobs. We could not control him, nor understand him. He went around healing people mysteriously, which was unnecessary. There is nothing in our rules about the necessity for helping others. He never stopped breaking our rules. We thought he was sent from the devil to destroy our system. He would never cooperate with us or yield to our authority. He crossed social barriers, which was totally wrong. People must stay in their place, as we Pharisees must stay in ours.

For example, he talked to a woman of questionable character in Samaria. Jews don't associate with Samaritans, let alone women. Then, this socially unacceptable woman went all over her village declaring that he was the promised Messiah. That's not rational. No Messiah would come to a woman alone and talk to her, or bother with someone so disliked. People became excited with what she said and there could have been a riot. He excited people like this. He also healed a blind man without our consent, and he did it on a day that was not in agreement with our system. We threw the healed man out of the synagogue for having had anything to do with Jesus. He was supposed to respect us first. We wanted to teach him and anyone else who associated with Jesus a good lesson about our power and place in society.

There were rumors that he fed thousands of people by the Sea of Galilee. Why? Why did he have to do that? He gathered all those people on the mountainside and then fed them. They became fascinated by him and after that, they wanted him to be their king. Again, he was trying to incite those people to rebellion and lead them away from us. He is full of deceptive tricks. I'd like to ask you when these magic signs and situations were going to stop. We don't need things like this in society. It gets people aggravated and out of control. Everything was perfectly fine before. Soon, I knew we had to try to take Jesus and totally destroy him before he destroyed us. We had no choice.

The Pharisees that turned away from us said that the Scriptures helped prove that he was the Jewish Messiah. They pointed out that the Prophet Zechariah said that the king would be humble and mounted on a donkey![1] Of course, a few days before Passover the man did ride into Jerusalem on a donkey. Locals spread out palm branches and hailed him as their king, but that doesn't mean much to me.

Some fellow colleagues mentioned the Prophet Micah in correlation to Jesus of Nazareth. Micah said that the Messiah would come from Bethlehem and go on to eternity.[2] Jesus evidently was born in Bethlehem and often does mention an eternal kingdom. Supposedly, when Jesus was born in Bethlehem, there was some type of commotion and excitement among local shepherds. They claimed at that time that they were told by angels about the baby Jesus who was born that night who would be their savior. Personally, I find that to be totally irrelevant. Who would consider valid the testimony of local shepherds? Who cares what they have to say? They are not important members of any society. If a Messiah were being born, our God Jehovah wouldn't deal with shepherds. He would have his angels tell us first, of course. Other rumors mentioned wise men from the East who risked their lives to find the baby Jesus in Bethlehem. No matter what, nothing has been proven about the prophecies and it still doesn't obliterate the fact that Jesus of Nazareth is an obstacle to the Jewish system and my future.

Still, other men mentioned the old Prophet Isaiah and a vague connection with eternity about which he wrote. They quoted,

*"For a child will be born to us, a son will be given to us,*
*And the government will rest on his shoulders,*
*And His name will be called Wonderful Counselor, Mighty God,*
*Eternal Father, Prince of Peace."*[3]

According to those Pharisees, Jesus represented overwhelming peace to them and they believed in eternity with him, also. I do not understand them, and consider them inadequate and lost as people. I don't need to dwell on their problems or think about them.

Since Jesus of Nazareth always eluded us when we tried to capture him, we thought of a plan. We decided to employ legions from the Roman army to take him prisoner during the night. The night would be the best for us because then none of the man's constituents would be able to interfere. We found a willing follower of his, Judas Iscariot, who easily was convinced to be paid to identify him in a set-up situation. We knew that Judas loved money and had a reputation for stealing from the disciples' treasury box. Our bargain was thirty pieces of silver to identify Jesus in the night. Judas couldn't have been a better contact man, and he molded easily to our desires. After Jesus had celebrated the Passover, he and his group of followers went into the Garden of Gethsemane. We wouldn't have known where to find the man, and Judas knew all the ins and outs of the disciples' activities. We had hundreds of armed soldiers ready in the background while we discreetly followed Judas. It all depended on him, because in the dark we wouldn't have been able to recognize Jesus accurately.

Judas approached his master with a kiss. We knew we had the Nazarene then and signaled the soldiers to surround the place. Ironically, he did not seem to fear us, but looked at us directly as though he were expecting us. That's not unusual for him. He usually detected when something important was going to happen. In this case, he did not appear to be disturbed at all. The soldiers were so shocked by his behavior that they fell back away from him in great fear. I noticed that one of the disciples took his sword and cut off the ear of my slave. That was uncalled for, but Jesus easily healed it. He was always doing things like that for no apparent reason. A slave has very little value. You can always get a slave. It wouldn't matter at all if his ear were cut off. The point is that Jesus wasn't supposed to do things like this without our permission and without regard to our rules.

We took him to private homes during the night and tried him three times. Finally, we found a legal crime of which we could accuse him, and then we sent him to Pilate the next morning. He claimed to be the Son of God, and this is blasphemy. Of course, he also was guilty of inciting riots among the people. No one could deny that. It was all neatly and conveniently done. Pilate didn't see things our way and sent him to Herod Antipas. Herod thought the whole thing foolish, but gave him a verdict of guilty to help Pilate. Pilate finally decided to exchange him with Barabbas and we cheered his decision. I can tell you we cheered with ecstasy.

He was nailed to the cross and left to die with the other criminals. I, for one, felt greatly relieved to know that our future would be safe again. There were thoughts presented by some of the Pharisees that he might somehow come back to life, so we decided to have his tomb well guarded. We paid the soldiers very well so nothing would happen. At least they'll do a good job. They respect us and our financial power. They know how important it is to have good pay.

Some people commented on the way that Jesus died and that it affected them deeply. Someone even mentioned that Jesus was the Son of God by the profundity of his death. Apparently, there was some importance of thought from the prisoner from the cross. He forgave everyone who was hurting him. That doesn't bother or even affect me. I'm an important Pharisee. Why would I need forgiveness? When the Messiah does come, I'm sure God will tell us first. This Jesus of Nazareth always helped and related to the poor and helpless. That doesn't make sense. Why would our God Jehovah send the Messiah to people who need so much help and have no importance?

I want things the way they used to be, and the way they're supposed to be. With Jesus in his grave, everything will soon be normal. People will forget all about him. They will come back to us and be devoted to us, the Pharisees. After all, this is a practical world we live in and Jesus of Nazareth was never practical for us. One has to protect one's own interests in this life. One has to be on top of things. Soon, it will be business as usual. *(Starts to go and then turns around slowly.)* And as I said, Jesus of Nazareth was never practical for us. He loved people and taught them about God and an eternal kingdom. That wasn't convenient with our religion, our lifestyle, or our personal interests. *(He slowly leaves.)*

The End

---

1. Zechariah 9:9

2. Micah 5:2

3. Isaiah 9:6

# 4

# The Passover Haggadah

A Traditional
Seder Service

*by*
**Robert L. Linder**
*and*
**Rabbi Sol Ester**

Reprinted from *The Passover – Haggadah,* published by CSS Publishing Company, Lima, Ohio.

# The Passover

"A program of fellowship for adults and/or youth in Christian congregations desiring a better understanding of the heritage and the meaning of the institution of the Sacrament of Holy Communion."

This work was inspired and initially written by Rev. Robert L. Linder while pastor of First English Lutheran Church in Toledo, Ohio. He was assisted by Jewish leaders of the community. It has since been revised by others, including Rabbi Sol Oster of Lima, Ohio.

| I. SANCTIFICATION of the Feast-day. | II. WASH the hands before the service. | III. KARPAS (Parsley, etc.) is now eaten. |
|---|---|---|
| IV. DIVIDE the middle of the three *Mazzoth*. | V. RECITE the account of the Exodus, the *Haggadah*. | VI. WASHING the hands once more, preparatory to the meal. |
| VII. GRACE before bread is now recited, before partaking of | VIII. MAZZAH, with its special benediction. | IX. BITTER HERB is now tasted: it is then |
| X. COMBINED with *Mazzah* and *Haroseth*, and eaten as one. | XI. TABLE IS SPREAD, and all partake of the meal, ending with | XII. THE HIDDEN MAZZAH, put on one side at the beginning of the service. |
| XIII. GRACE after the meal is then recited, followed by | XIV. HALLEL, the Psalms of Praise. | XV. ACCEPTED be our service before God! |

# THE TRADITIONAL ORDER OF THE SEDER SERVICE

## BLESSING OF THE FESTIVAL CANDLES

*Before sunset and prior to sitting down for the Seder, the mother and daughters light the candles and pray:*

Our God and God of our fathers, may the rays of these festival candles cast their glow upon the earth and bring the radiance of Thy divine light to all who still dwell in darkness and in bondage. May this season marking the deliverance of our ancestors from Pharaoh arouse us against any despot who keeps man bowed in servitude. In gratitude for the freedom which is ours, may we strive to bring about the liberation of all humankind. Bless our home and our dear ones with the light of Thy spirit. Amen.

*****

## THE HAGGADAH
## THE MESSAGE OF PASSOVER

**Leader**

Welcome to our Seder! Tonight we observe a most ancient, colorful, and significant festival. The Seder takes us back to those events which occurred more than three thousand years ago. We recall the Egyptian bondage of the Children of Israel and their deliverance by God.

History tells us that many other peoples were also enslaved by tyrants. But the Israelites were the first to rebel against serfdom, and to institute a holiday dedicated to freedom. Most nations observe an Independence Day, but the observance of the birthday of Jewish freedom is unique because of its profoundly religious character. Every Jewish home becomes a sanctuary, every table and altar a place where gratitude is expressed to God, the Author of liberty. Through prayer and song, ritual and symbol, custom and ceremony, we look upon ourselves as though we were among those enslaved and then brought forth unto freedom.

This self-dedication with the past of our people helps us better to appreciate the freedom that is ours, and more fully to understand the plight of such of our brethren as still dwell under the shadow of tyrants. The Seder calls upon us to do all in our power to emancipate them from tyranny.

The Seder, which keeps alive in us the love of liberty, has a significance also for all humankind. Freedom, which is one of man's most precious gifts, must not be taken for granted. In every age it must be won anew. The Pharaoh of the Exodus is symbolic of the tyrants of our day as well as of the tyrants in every era of history.

If a people is anywhere exploited and oppressed, then nowhere is man really secure. Freedom is indivisible. The Seder expresses the need of man's eternal vigilance in the struggle to preserve and advance the cause of freedom and human dignity. May God grant that the freedom which prevails here in our beloved land shall become the blessed lot of all the children of men.

1. KADDESH — Sanctify the Name of God

Fill the First Cup of Wine

Leader

We begin this service by sanctifying the name of God and proclaiming the holiness of this Festival. Wine in the East is as common a beverage as tea and coffee are for us. With a blessing over wine, the Jew ushers in the Sabbath and all Festivals. The Kiddush ceremonial, invoking God while partaking of wine, may be one of the reasons why the traditional Jew developed temperance and sobriety. With this cup of wine, symbol of joy, let us now usher in our inspiring Festival of Passover.

In Unison

Our God and God of our fathers, we thank Thee that Thou hast enabled us to gather in happy fellowship, again to observe the Festival of Freedom. Just as for many centuries the Seder has brought together families and friends to retell the events which led to our freedom, so may we this night be at one with Jews everywhere who perform this ancient ritual linking us with our historic past. As we relive each event in our people's ancient struggle, and celebrate their emergence from slavery to freedom, we pray that all of us may keep alive in our hearts the love of liberty. May we dedicate our lives to the abolition of all forms of tyranny and injustice.

As we partake of this cup of wine, symbol of joy, we acknowledge Thee our Creator, our Father, our Liberator. We praise Thy holy name in the traditional words of the Kiddush:

*Praised be Thou, O Lord our God,*
*King of the Universe,*
*Creator of the fruit of the vine.*

*Praised be Thou, O Lord our God, King of the Universe, who didst choose us from among all people for Thy service, and exalted us by teaching us holiness through Thy commandments. Out of love hast Thou given us, O Lord our God, holidays for gladness, festivals and seasons for rejoicing, among them this day of the Feast of Unleavened Bread, the season of our freedom, a festival of holy assembly, commemorating our liberation from Egypt. From among all peoples hast Thou chosen us, and didst sanctify us by giving us Thy holy festivals as a joyous heritage. Praised be Thou, O Lord, who hallowest Israel and the festivals.*

She-he-he-ya-nu

*Praised be Thou, O Lord our God, King of the Universe, who hast kept us in life and sustained us, and enabled us to reach this season.*

Drink the First Cup of Wine
Lean to the Left

## 2. u-r'HATZ — Wash the Hands

It was an ancient custom in the East, especially among Jews, to wash their hands before eating. A pitcher of water with basin and towels may be passed around to the guests or, to save time, several containers of water and basins may be set at convenient places on the table.

### Wash the Hands

### 3. KARPAS — Eat a Green Vegetable

The green vegetable is a symbol of springtime and the miracle of nature's renewal. At this season when Mother Earth arrays herself in fresh verdure, the spirit of man rises, and he renews his faith in a world where freedom and justice will prevail.

The salt water, into which the Karpas is dipped to make it palatable, has been interpreted as salty tears, to remind us of the tears shed by the oppressed Israelites.

Before partaking of the Karpas, recite the following blessing:

*Praised be Thou, O Lord our God,*
*King of the Universe,*
*Creator of the fruit of the Earth.*

### Eat the Vegetable

### 4. YAHATZ — Break the Middle of the Three Matzot

For the daily meal, there is one loaf of bread; but on the Sabbath there are two loaves as a reminder of the double portion of manna which fell on Friday for the Children of Israel as they traveled in the wilderness (Exodus 16:22). In honor of Passover, a third matzah was added specifically for the Seder.

When the Temple was in existence, special food, considered sacred, was eaten by the Kohanim and the L'vi-yim. But the Passover indicates that all Jews are united in a covenant of equality. To demonstrate this pattern of democracy, everyone at the Seder will tonight partake of all three matzot.

The middle matzah is broken into two pieces. The smaller half is replaced on the Seder plate to be used later for the Ha-Motzi.

The larger half is wrapped in a napkin, as a symbol of the unleavened dough, to be eaten as the Afikoman at the end of the meal. The Host, or Leader, asks the children to close their eyes as he hides the Afikoman. Anyone finding it may claim a reward because the meal cannot be ritually completed without the Afikoman.

Break Into 2 Pieces Middle Matzot
Hide Afikoman (Give to Adult Member)

5. MAGGID — Tell the Story of the Exodus

Hospitality is a time-honored virtue among our people. The custom of inviting to the Seder all who are hungry originated in Babylonia. Therefore the invitation is expressed not in Hebrew but in Aramaic, the language then current. Our Seder would not be true to tradition unless we offer hospitality to any stranger in our midst, or make it possible for the needy to observe their own Seder.

As a sign of hospitality, the door is opened
Have a Young Man Open a Door in Fellowship Hall

The Leader uncovers the Matzah,
Lifts up the Ceremonial Plate and says:

*Behold the Matzah, bread of poverty, which our ancestors ate in the land of Egypt.*

*Let all who are hungry come and eat; All who are needy, come and celebrate the Passover with us.*

*Now we are here: Next year may we observe the Passover in the land of Israel.*

*Now many are still enslaved: Next year may all men be free.*

(The Haggadah, the dramatic portrayal of the exodus from Egyptian bondage, is for the entire family. Being child-centered, it encourages especially the children to ask questions concerning the ritual and meaning of the service. The Seder brings families together and strengthens the bonds of Jewish family solidarity.)

After the door has been closed, the wine cup is filled the second time, and the youngest child, or a guest, asks the Four Questions.

## THE FOUR QUESTIONS

### WHY IS THIS NIGHT DIFFERENT FROM ALL OTHER NIGHTS?

*(1) On all other nights we may eat either leavened or unleavened bread, but on this night we eat only the unleavened bread.*

*(2) On all other nights we eat all kinds of herbs, but on this night we eat especially bitter herbs.*

*(3) On all other nights, we need not even once dip our herbs in any condiment, but on this night we dip herbs twice: one herb in salt water, and the bitter herbs in Haroset.*

*(4) On all other nights we eat either sitting or reclining, but on this night we recline.*

Leader
Before we read the Haggadah, which tells in detail the whole story, let me answer your questions one by one:
(1) We eat matzah because, when our ancestors were told by Pharaoh that they could leave Egypt, they had no time to bake bread with leaven, so they baked it without leaven.
(2) At the Seder, we eat bitter herbs to remind us of the bitterness our ancestors experienced when they were oppressed by the Egyptian taskmaster.
(3) At the Seder, we dip food twice; the parsley in salt water, as we have already explained, and the bitter herbs in Haroset, as we shall later explain.
(4) As a sign of freedom, we lean to the left when we partake of wine and symbolic food. In antiquity, slaves ate hurriedly, standing

or squatting on the ground, while royalty, nobility, and the wealthy in Egypt, Persia, Rome, and other empires dined on couches. To indicate that the ancient Israelites were now free, they too reclined while eating. Since it is impractical for each person to have a dining couch, only the Leader is provided with pillows on which to lean, and the rest lean to the left when drinking the wine and eating the matzah.

Now let us return to the text of the Haggadah for the details as to why this night is different from all other nights.

*We were once the slaves of Pharaoh in Egypt, but the Lord our God brought us forth from there with a mighty hand and an outstretched arm (Deuteronomy 6:21; 26:8). Had not the Holy One, praised be He, brought our fathers out of Egypt, then we and our children and our children's children might still be enslaved to a pharaoh in Egypt. Therefore, even if all of us were endowed with wisdom and understanding, and all of us thoroughly versed in the Torah, it would nevertheless be our duty to tell of the Exodus from Egypt. And to dwell at length on the story of the liberation is indeed praiseworthy.*

*We are told that Rabbi Eliezer, Rabbi Joshua, Rabbi Elazar, son of Azariah, Rabbi Akiba, and Rabbi Tarfon sat at the Seder table in B'nai B'rak and, the whole night through, discussed the liberation from Egypt until their disciples came in and said: "Rabbis! It is now time to recite the Shema of the morning prayers."*

*Rabbi Elazar, son of Azariah, said, "I am nearly seventy years old, yet I never could understand why the Exodus from Egypt should also be mentioned in the evening service, until Ben Zoma explained it by quoting the verse: 'That you may remember the day you went forth from Egypt all the days of your life' (Deuteronomy 16:3). The days of your life would imply the daytime only. All the days of your life includes the nights also." There is, however, another explanation given by the sages: "The days of your life refers to this world. All the days of your life includes also the messianic era."*

*Praised be God: Praised be He: Praised be He who gave the Torah to his people Israel: Praised be He.*

# THE FOUR SONS

*The Torah speaks of four types of children: one who is wise, one who is rebellious, one who is simple, and one who does not know how to ask.*

*The wise son asks, "What is the meaning of the laws, regulations and ordinances which the Lord our God has commanded you?" (Deuteronomy 6:20).* To him you shall explain all the laws of Passover even to the last detail, that nothing may be eaten and no entertainment or revelry is to take place after the *Afikoman*.

*The rebellious son asks, "What does this service mean to you?" (Exodus 12:26).* By using the expression "to you," it is evident that this service has no significance for him. He has thus excluded himself from his people and denied God; therefore, give him a caustic answer and say: "It is because of what the Lord did for me when I came out of Egypt" (Exodus 13:8). "For me," not for him, for had he been there in Egypt, he would not have deserved to be liberated.

*The simple son asks: "What does this mean?"* Tell him, "With a mighty hand, the Lord brought us out of Egypt, out of the house of bondage" (Exodus 13:14).

*As for the one who does not know how to ask,* begin by explaining, as we are told: "You shall tell your son on that day, 'I do this because of what the Lord did for me when I came out of Egypt'" (Exodus 13:8).

One might think that the Haggadah should be recited beginning with the first day of the month of Nisan. But the Bible says: "You shall tell your son on that day," (the fifteenth day of Nisan, the first day of Passover). One might infer "on that day" means in the daytime. But the verse continues: "I do this because of what the Lord did for me when I came out of Egypt," namely in the evening, when the Matzah and Bitter Herbs are actually placed before you.

In the beginning (before the days of Abraham), our forefathers were idol worshipers. God, however, called us to His service. For so we read in the Torah: "And Joshua said unto all the people, 'thus said the Lord, God of Israel: In the days of old, your fathers, even Terah, the father of Abraham and Nahor, lived beyond the

River Euphrates, and they worshiped idols. But I took your father, Abraham, from beyond the River Euphrates and I led him through the entire land of Canaan. I multiplied his offspring and gave him Isaac. To Isaac I gave Jacob and Esau. To Esau I gave Mount Seir as an inheritance: but Jacob and his sons went down into Egypt' " (Joshua 24:2-4).

Praised be God who keeps His promise to Israel: Praised be He! For the Holy One, praised be He, determined the end of our bondage in order to fulfill His word, pledged in a solemn covenant to our father Abraham: "And God said to Abraham, 'Know this for certain: your descendants shall be strangers in a land not their own, where they shall be enslaved and oppressed for four hundred years. But I will also bring judgment on the nation that held them in slavery: and in the end they shall go free with great substance' " (Genesis 15:13-14).

Raise the Cup of Wine and Cover the Matzot

*God's unfailing help has sustained our fathers and us. For not only one enemy has risen up to destroy us, but in every generation do men rise up against us seeking to destroy us: but the Holy One, praised be He, delivers us from their hands.*

The Cup of Wine is Set Down on the Table and the Matzot are Uncovered

We must be on guard against two kinds of enemies who would deprive us of our freedom: (1) the enemy without, easily recognized by his malicious words and evil deeds; and (2) the enemy within, posing as a friend and betraying us. Pharaoh was the enemy without and Laban, referred to in the passage which follows, symbolized the treacherous, false friend.

*Let us analyze, for instance, what Laban, the Aramean (Syrian), intended to do to Jacob, our father. Whereas Pharaoh issued a decree against newborn males only, Laban sought to annihilate Jacob and his entire family, for the Biblical verse may be read: "The Aramean wanted to destroy my father."*

> With a Small Spoon, Spill from Your Cup
> Some Wine for Each of the Three Miracles
> as Each Miracle is Mentioned

*"Blood, fire, and pillars of smoke."* (Joel 3:3).

As we read in the Haggadah about plague after plague, with a small spoon we spill some wine into our plate.

> With a Small Spoon, Spill into Your Plate
> Some of the Wine as Each Plague is Mentioned

*These were the Ten Plagues which the Holy One, praised be He, brought upon the Egyptians in Egypt:*

(1) Blood, (2) Frogs, (3) Vermin, (4) Wild Beasts, (5) Cattle Disease, (6) Boils, (7) Hail, (8) Locusts, (9) Darkness, (10) Smiting of the First-born.

## DAYYENU

At this point in the Seder a hymn is sung called Dayyenu, a rising crescendo of thanksgiving, beginning with gratitude for physical deliverance, and ending with gratitude for the spiritual blessings of the Sabbath and the Torah.

> Sing the Doxology —
> "Praise God From Whom All Blessings Flow"

> One of the participants asks:
> 1st Male Adult

*What is the meaning of the Paschal Lamb which our forefathers used to eat at the time when the Temple was still in existence?*

> The Leader points to the shank bone of the lamb
> and answers:

*The Paschal Lamb is to remind us that the Holy One, praised* be He, passed over the houses of our forefathers in Egypt, as it is written in the Bible: "You shall say that it is the sacrifice of the Lord's Passover, for He passed over the houses of the children of Israel in Egypt when He smote the Egyptians, but spared our houses. The people bowed their heads and worshiped" (Exodus 12:27).

One of the participants asks:
2nd Male Adult
*What is the meaning of the Matzah that we eat?*

The Leader raises the Matzah and answers:
*The Matzah is to remind us that before the dough which our forefathers prepared for bread had time to ferment, the supreme King of kings, the Holy One, praised be He, revealed himself to them and redeemed them. We read in the Bible, "They baked Matzah of the unleavened dough which they had brought out of Egypt, for it had not leavened because they were thrust out of Egypt and could not linger, nor had they prepared any food for the journey" (Exodus 12:30).*

One of the participants asks:
3rd Male Adult
*What is the meaning of the bitter herbs which we eat?*

The Leader points to the Maror and answers:
*The Maror is to remind us that the Egyptians embittered the lives of our forefathers in Egypt, as the Bible explains: "They made their lives bitter with hard labor, with mortar and brick, and with every kind of work in the field. All the labor which the Egyptians forced upon them was harsh" (Exodus 1:14).*

*In every generation each Jew should regard himself as though he personally went forth from Egypt. That is what the Bible means when it says: "And you shall tell your son on that day, saying, 'It is because of what the Lord did for me when I went forth from Egypt'" (Exodus 13:8). It was not only our forefathers whom the Holy One, praised be He, redeemed from slavery, but us also did He redeem together with them, as we read: "He brought us out from there so that He might bring us into the land, and give us this land which he promised to our forefathers" (Deuteronomy 6:23).*

*Therefore we should thank and praise, laud and glorify, exalt and honor, extol and adore God who performed all these miracles for our fathers and for us. He brought us from slavery to freedom, from sorrow to joy, from mourining to festivity, from darkness to great light, and from bondage to redemption. Let us, then, sing unto Him a new song: Halleluyah, praise the Lord!*

## HALLEL

The following psalm in the Hallel is the same one as the Levites chanted in the Temple when the Paschal sacrifices were offered.

### When Israel Went Forth From Egypt
### Responsive Reading

### Psalm 114

When Israel went forth from Egypt,
    The house of Jacob from a people
    of strange language,
R: Judah became his sanctuary,
    Israel his dominion.

The sea looked and fled,
    Jordan turned back.
R: The mountains skipped like rams,
    the hills like lambs.

What ails you, O sea, that you flee?
O Jordan, that you turn back?
R: O mountains, that you skip like rams?
    O hills, like lambs?

> Tremble, O earth, at the presence of the Lord
> at the presence of the God of Jacob,
> R: who turns the rock into a pool of water,
> the flint into a spring of water.

Participants raise their second cup of wine

*Praised be Thou, O Lord our God, King of the Universe, who redeemed us, and redeemed our fathers from Egypt, and enabled us to reach this night on which we eat Matzah and Maror. Even so, O Lord our God and God of our fathers, do Thou enable us to reach in peace other holy days and festivals when we may rejoice in the restoration of Zion, Thy city, and find delight in serving Thee. There we shall partake of the Paschal meal and bring Thee the offerings which shall be acceptable unto Thee. And there we shall sing unto Thee a new song of praise for our freedom and redemption. Praised be Thou, O Lord, Redeemer of Israel.*

*Praised be Thou, O Lord our God,*
*King of the Universe,*
*Creator of the fruit of the vine.*

After the blessing, drink this second cup
of wine while reclining to the left

### 6. RAHATZ — Wash the Hands Before the Meal

### 7. MOTZI — Say the HA-MOTZI

*Praised be Thou, O Lord our God, King of the Universe, who bringest forth sustenance from the Earth.*

### 8. MATZAH — Recite the Blessing for the Matzah

*Praised be Thou, O Lord our God, King of the Universe, who has sanctified us with Thy commandments and enjoined upon us the Mitzvah of eating unleavened bread.*

## 9. MAROR — Eat the Bitter Herbs

The bitter herbs of which we shall partake are a reminder of the bitterness the Israelites experienced in Egypt. The Haroset into which the bitter herbs are dipped symbolizes the mortar and bricks with which our forefathers were forced to construct cities and treasure-houses for Pharaoh.

Life is bittersweet. The sweet and pleasant taste of the Haroset impresses upon us that, no matter how bitter and dark the present appears, we should hopefully look forward to better days. "Sweet are the uses of adversity."

A portion of the bitter herbs is dipped into the Haroset and eaten by each one present after reciting the following blessing:

*Praised be Thou, O Lord our God, King of the Universe, who hast sanctified us by Thy commandments and enjoined upon us the Mitzvah of eating the Bitter Herbs.*

Eat Bitter Herbs

## 10. KOREKH — Eat the Matzah and Maror Sandwich

The bottom matzah is broken into small pieces. Each person receives two pieces between which are placed some of the bitter herbs.

*As a reminder of the Temple, we follow the practice of Hillel*

*While the Temple was still in existence, Hillel would eat together in a sandwich some Matzah and Maror, to fulfill the biblical command: "They shall eat it (the Paschal Lamb) together with unleavened bread and bitter herbs" (Numbers 9:11).*

All eat the Matzah and Maror Sandwich

11. SHULHAN OREKH — Take time to Enjoy the Festival Meal
(the Carry-in Dinner)
(Symbol of the Festival Meal — Walnuts and Apples
Ground Fine, add Cinnamon and enough Wine to Moisten)

Now that we have completed the first part of the Haggadah, we are ready for the Passover meal. When the Temple was in existence, roasted lamb was eaten at the Seder. Since the destruction of the Temple, lamb is not served, and nothing is included in the meal that has been roasted on an open flame.

Remove the ritual symbols from the table.

In many homes, it is customary to begin the meal with a hard-boiled egg, usually dipped in salt water. Three interesting explanations are given for this practice. First, unlike most foods which become softer, the more it is boiled, the harder the egg becomes. This indicates the stubborn resistance of the Jews to those who sought to crush them. Secondly, the egg is regarded as the symbol of new life; a chick must break its egg to emerge into life. Finally, since the roasted egg on the Seder plate is a reminder of the sacrifice that took place in the Temple of old, we eat the egg to remind us of the destruction of the Temple and of our obligation to aid in the rebuilding of Zion today.

12. TZAFUN

Since the meal cannot be ritually completed without eating the Afikoman, the Leader or Host now calls for the Afikoman (the portion of the middle matzah that was hidden). The child who finds it receives a reward. The Afikoman is our substitute for the Paschal Lamb, which in days of old was the final food of the Seder feast.

Take time to enjoy and eat the Afikoman

13. BAREKH — Recite the Birkat Hamazon
(Blessing after the meal)

It is appropriate to introduce the Birkat Hamazon with the singing of Psalm 126, which describes the great joy of the exiles, twenty-five hundred years ago, when they returned from Babylonia to Zion. Throughout the ages, this same psalm brought hope to the Jews that Zion would be restored and provide a homeland for the homeless and oppressed of their people.

When the Lord restored the
    fortunes of Zion,
we were like those who dream.
Then our mouth was filled with
    laughter,
    and our tongue with shouts of joy;
then they said among the nations,
    "The Lord has done great things for them."
The Lord has done great things for us,
    we are glad.

Restore our fortunes, O Lord,
    like the water-courses in the Negeb!
May those who sow in tears
    reap with shouts of joy!
He that goes forth weeping,
    bearing the seed for sowing,
shall come home with shouts of joy,
    bringing his sheaves with him.

Leader
*Let us say the blessing for our food.*

Participants, and then Leader
*Praised be the name of the Lord
from this time forth and forever.*

Leader
*With the permission of those present, let us
praise Him (our God) of whose bounty we have partaken.*

*Participants, then Leader*
*Praised be He (our God) of whose bounty we have partaken and through whose goodness we live.*

Drink the third cup of wine while leaning to the left

*Praised be Thou, O Lord our God,
King of the Universe,
Creator of the fruit of the vine.*

The fourth cup of wine is filled
The chalice for Elijah is also filled with wine

Among the awaited guests is the prophet Elijah who, according to tradition, never died, but was carried up to heaven. The life of no other character in Jewish history is so surrounded with a halo of mystery and wonder as is that of Elijah. In Jewish legend, the ubiquitous Elijah is the champion of the oppressed; he brings hope, cheer and relief to the downtrodden; and he performs miracles of rescue and deliverance.

It is Elijah who can explain all difficult passages in the Bible and Talmud and will settle all future controversies. The prophet Malachi says of him: "He will turn the hearts of parents to their children, and the hearts of children to their parents." Elijah is the harbinger of good tidings of joy and peace. His name is especially associated with the coming of the Messiah, whose advent he is expected to announce.

Let us open the door and rise in the hope that Elijah will enter. With the salutation reserved for distinguished guests, let us say:

Boy opens door

*Blessed be he who comes in the name of the Lord.*

*Elijah, the prophet, Elijah, the Tishbite:
Elijah, the Gileadite:
May he soon come and bring the Messiah.*

The door is closed

Leader
Let us now pause to recall the bitter catastrophe which so recently has befallen our people in Europe.

Responsive Reading
When in the past our brothers were massacred in ruthless pogroms, the poet Bialik, in his "City of Slaughter," cried out against this bloody savagery.

> R: Today we mourn, not for one "city of slaughter" but for many such cities where six million of our people have been brutally destroyed.

The cruelties of Pharaoh, Haban, Nebuchadnezzar, and Titus cannot be compared to the diabolical devices fashioned by modern tyrants in their design to exterminate a whole people.

> R: No generation has known a catastrophe so vast and tragic!

The blood of the innocent, who perished in the gas-chambers of Auschwitz, Bergen-Belsen, Buchenwald, Dachau, Majdanek, Treblinka, and Theresienstadt, cries out to God and to man.

> R: How can we ever forget the burning of synagogues and houses of study, the destruction of the holy books and scrolls of the Torah, the sadistic torment and murder of our scholars, sages, and teachers?

They tortured the flesh of our brothers, but they could not crush their spirit, their faith, nor their love of Torah.

> R: The parchment of the Torah was burnt, but the letters were indestructible.

In the Warsaw Ghetto, Jews valiantly defied the overwhelming forces of the inhuman tyrant. Those martyrs lifted up their voices in a hymn reaffirming their faith in the coming of the Messiah, when justice and peace shall finally be established for all men.

> R: "I believe with a perfect faith in the coming of the Messiah; and though he tarry, nonetheless do I believe he will come!"

Let us pray: O Lord, remember Thy martyred children; remember all who have given their lives for Kiddush Hashem, the sanctification of Thy name.

> R: Grant their souls the peace reserved for all the righteous who are in Thy tender keeping.

And as we mourn Israel's tragic fate, we also recall with admiration and gratitude the compassionate men and women of other faiths and nationalities who, at the peril of their lives, protected and saved thousands of Jews.

> R: They are among those whom our Rabbis had in mind when they taught: "The righteous of all nations have a share in the world to come."

We are grateful to all the Allied Nations who liberated our people, and people of other faiths, from Nazi imprisonment, torture, and death.

> R: With thankful hearts we shall ever remember the care and encouragement they gave to all those who were tragically displaced.

Let us all pray and work together for that day when there shall be no more violence or desolation anywhere on this earth.

> R: "Nation shall not lift sword against nation; neither shall they learn war anymore."

We who have witnessed the darkest chapter in modern Jewish history have also witnessed our people's greatest triumph: the rebirth of the Jewish State.

> R: We thank Thee, O Lord, that Thou hast permitted us to behold our people's return to Zion.

Thou has opened the gates, and Thou didst "bring the remnant of Thy people from the east, and didst gather them from the west; Thou didst say to the north 'Give up!' and to the south 'Do not withhold them!' "

> R: "Thou didst bring Thy sons from afar, and Thy daughters from the ends of the earth!"

May we who live in this land of freedom help our brothers to rebuild the State of Israel, that it may become secure and self-supporting, a stronghold of democracy, a bridge which unites the peoples of the East and of the West.

> R: "For out of Zion shall go forth the Torah, and the word of God from Jerusalem."

## 14. HALLEL

Hallel (Psalms of Praise) precedes and follows the festive meal to indicate that the meal is part of the religious service. Eating is not the mere consumption of food. In Judaism, the family meal is sanctified with prayer and D'VAR TORAH.

Recite the Hallel (Psalm 117)

> Praise the Lord, all nations!
> Extol him, all peoples!
> For great is his steadfast love toward us:
>    and the faithfulness of the Lord
>    endures forever.
> Praise the Lord!

## Prayer closing the Hallel

*All Thy words shall praise Thee, O Lord our God, and Thy pious ones, the just who do Thy will, together with all Thy people, the house of Israel, shall praise Thee in joyous song. They shall thank, exalt, revere and sanctify Thee, and ascribe sovereignty to Thy name, O our King. For it is good to give thanks to Thee, and it is fitting to sing praises to Thy name, for Thou art God from everlasting to everlasting.*

## The Fourth Cup of Wine

There are several explanations why we drink four cups of wine at the Seder. The four cups correspond to the four letters of God's name: YOD HEH VAV HEH (Jehovah) — to indicate that God, the Liberator, is the Author of our freedom.

They mark the four divisions of the Seder service: the Kiddush; the reading of the Haggadah; the Birkat Hamazon (blessing after the meal); and the concluding psalms and prayers.

The Bible uses four different expressions for the redemption of the Israelites from Egyptian bondage.

After reciting the following blessing,
drink the fourth cup of wine while reclining.

*Praised be Thou, O Lord our God,
King of the Universe,
Creator of the fruit of the vine.*

## 15. NIRTZAH — Conclude the Seder

The following verses are from the conclusion of the PIYYUT that enumerated all the regulations of the Seder.

ALL:

*Now is our Seder concluded,
Each custom and law fulfilled:*

*As we gathered to celebrate a Seder this night,
May we be worthy in freedom next year
Again to celebrate a Seder.*

*O Pure One, who dwellest on high,
Raise up Thy numberless flock,
Speedily lead Thou the shoots of Thy stock
Redeemed, to Zion with song.*

*Next year in Jerusalem!*

The service could be concluded by offering the sacrament of Holy Communion with bread and chalice.

# 5

# A Good Friday Vigil

Service Of Scripture
And Meditation

*by*
*Alexander H. Wales*

# A Good Friday Vigil

The following service is useful in a small room setting, establishing a "come and go" time frame for worshipers to contemplate the events of Good Friday in a personal, meditative manner. The brief service is intended to last approximately fifteen minutes, with worshipers choosing to stay for as long a time as their schedule and lifestyle allow for personal prayer and meditation. It originally was created for use at the end of the school/work day and prior to a family mealtime, but could also be used at a midday/lunchtime setting.

A small room, with a capacity of ten to twenty individuals, is lighted with several candles, with a worship center created by a crown of thorns, a cross and a Christ Candle. The room is lighted only by candles. Care must be taken with the placement of the candles to prevent fire hazard, and for the movement of worshipers and leaders.

Beside the worship center, a prerecorded tape of sacred music (in our case, a collection of Gregorian chants and quiet, meditative organ music) is played during the gathering time and after the readings are completed. The combination of candlelight and music creates a wonderful atmosphere suitable to the Good Friday setting.

A worship leader is designated as reader for this service and is in charge of candle lighting and extinguishing.

The **service begins** with the **playing** of the **taped music** and **lighting** of all the **candles** in the room (usually eight to twelve candles and the Christ Candle). A grouping of three candles serves as "reading light" for the worship leader.

After worshipers are seated, the **worship leader reads**: Luke 22:39-48, 52-71.

Pause for **silent meditation** and **prayer** after extinguishing one of the three reading candles.

The **worship leader** then **reads:** Matthew 27:1-5 and Mark 15:6-20.

Pause for **silent meditation** and **prayer** after extinguishing one of the remaining two reading candles.

The **worship leader** then **reads:** Luke 23:26-27, 32-34, 39-46 and Mark 15:39, 42-47.

Pause for **silent meditation** and **prayer** after extinguishing the final reading candle and all but a few of the remaining candles at the back of the room.

Then **read:** "He was in the world, and the world knew him not."

Snuff out the Christ Candle.

Rewind the tape and begin again on the hour and the half hour, providing four worship sessions over a two-hour period. This may be extended to a third hour if enough worshipers are present or a longer time for individuals to participate is needed.

# 6

## Shadows Around The Cross

### A Tenebrae

### by
### Ralph Dessem

Reprinted from *Shadows Around The Cross,* published by CSS Publishing Company, Lima, Ohio.

# Introduction

## The Tenebrae Tradition

It has become traditional in many churches to present a Tenebrae Service on Good Friday, or at some other time during Holy Week. The tradition goes back to at least the eighth century; the service is presented as a ceremony that progresses from light to dark. The word *tenebrae* is a Latin term and is literally translated as "shadows." As each candle is extinguished in this service, it symbolizes the various shadows that surrounded Jesus and his cross just prior to his death.

## The Purpose

This service is designed so that each worshiper will re-examine his own spiritual life as it progresses from light to darkness. As he becomes mindful of those followers who fell away, and of those who were antagonistic and cruel to Jesus, he ought to reflect upon his own sinfulness. Perhaps he has helped to crucify Christ anew by doing some of the same types of evil deeds. The service should end with each person in the pew having received a new appreciation of Christ and the gift of salvation.

## Suggested Uses

Good Friday evening is the time when this service can be used most effectively. This is when most congregations are in the best psychological mood for this type of ceremony. However, it can also be used very effectively on Good Friday afternoon, perhaps as a community service from 1 to 2 p.m. Some pastors will want to use this service on Maundy Thursday evening and follow it with Holy Communion. Since the sections of the service are not all related to the death of Jesus on the cross, it could be broken up and used in segments. For example, one portion could be used for brief devotions at each midweek Lenten service, or it could be used by a youth group for a series of Sunday evening devotions.

## The Setting

A very simple setting would be to use a seven-branch candelabra, with an acolyte extinguishing one candle at each portion of the service. In a church with a divided chancel, two candelabras and two acolytes can be most effective. A very impressive setting can be staged with a large wood cross in the front of the sanctuary. This could easily be constructed out of 2 x 6's and stained brown. The upright piece should be about 6 feet long, with a 4 foot cross arm. Drill seven holes in the cross, but at an angle. You may prefer to fasten small triangular blocks of wood to the cross, and drill the holes in these blocks. The cross, with the candles, should be braced from behind so that it can be displayed at an angle; this angle should be such that the candles will stand upright for burning during the service. The acolyte should begin to extinguish them at the bottom and move upward.

## The Participants

The pastor can present the entire tenebrae service, with the assistance of a choir and acolytes. However, it can be more effective if it is done by a group of seven narrators, such as laymen or youth. If this plan is used, the entire service should be rehearsed well in advance of the presentation.

## Alternate Ending

The service can be very effective if it ends with the seventh candle being extinguished during the singing of "In The Cross Of Christ I Glory." However, some pastors may desire to light a candle and place it on the altar in anticipation of the resurrection of Christ. The alternate ending is designed for this purpose, and will also remind the worshipers that Christ again reigns as the light of the world.

# The Service Of Tenebrae

## The Prelude

## The Call To Worship

**Minister:** Let us praise God for the gift of his Son who became the light of the world.

**Congregation:** We would thank him that Christ came as a great light shining into a world darkened with sin.

**Minister:** Let us never forget those shadows of evil which followed him to the cross.

**Congregation:** We would remember that the power of Christ is greater than the power of evil and will eventually overcome it.

## The Invocation *(In unison)*

Father, help us to be ever aware of those events that caused Jesus to be taken to the cross. As we become mindful of those who confronted him with betrayal, denial, rejection, injustice, torture, ridicule, and mockery, we realize that these same traits might be found in our lives. Help us to re-examine our inner selves in this hour, as we reflect upon the lives of those who failed our Savior. If we have crucified him anew, grant us forgiveness and cleanse our lives of sin. Uplift us that we might see beyond the shadows of the cross, and find the spirit of him who came as the light of the world, Jesus Christ our Lord. Amen.

## The Hymn Of Faith

"My Faith Looks Up To Thee" (Olivet)

My faith looks up to Thee,
Thou Lamb of Calvary,
Savior divine!
Now hear me while I pray,

Take all my guilt away,
O let me from this day
Be wholly Thine!

May thy rich grace impart
Strength to my fainting heart,
My zeal inspire;
As Thou hast died for me,
O may my love to Thee
Pure, warm and changeless be,
A living fire! Amen.

## The Shadow Of Betrayal

**The Scripture Reading**                      Matthew 26:47-50

While he was still speaking, Judas came, one of the twelve, and with him a great crowd with swords and clubs, from the chief priests and the elders of the people. Now the betrayer had given them a sign, saying, "The one I shall kiss is the man; seize him."

And he came up to Jesus at once and said, "Hail, Master!" And he kissed him. Jesus said to him, "Friend, why are you here?" Then they came up and laid hands on Jesus and seized him.

**The Meditation**

What was it that caused Judas to betray the one he had followed for almost three years? Why was Jesus betrayed by goodness into the hands of evil? One thing is certain: Judas performed his cruel act for more than just thirty pieces of silver.

Judas thought largely of himself. He had visualized himself in a position of great importance in the coming kingdom, and he felt his fond ambitions were being dashed to pieces by the delay of Jesus. Thus, he tried to force the hand of Jesus into setting up his kingdom immediately. When he thought of this new kingdom, Judas saw it from his own viewpoint and did not endeavor to discover the details of Jesus' view. The differences in the type of kingdom to be established gradually created a gulf between Judas and his Lord. His zeal for moving into a materialistic kingdom was so great that his zeal became misplaced when he entered into the deal with the enemies of Jesus.

Judas failed to anticipate the outcome of his evil deed before he did it. When he kissed the Master it had far-reaching effects. It was the signal that began the events that led to his death. Through this act, he actually sold his Lord into the hands of his enemies. But, he did more than that; he also sold himself and bought his own destruction.

The clouds over the Garden of Gethsemane now began to change in the moonlight; as they did so, they cast a cruel shadow around the Son of God and his followers.

Do you think of someone who has betrayed the Christ? Have you done so yourself, with your own selfishness?

Perhaps you have been an active witness to him through your church, but now you are beginning to have doubts concerning the mission and purpose of the Church. Will you continue to be faithful, or will you betray him as you let the spark of his spirit burn out without you?

## The Prayer

Lord, forgive us for our manifold sins; most of all forgive us when we have betrayed You. Turn not from us, even though we may have turned from You. By the power of your Spirit, cleanse us and renew us from within, in the name of Christ. Amen.

*(The first candle is extinguished)*

### The Shadow of Denial

## The Hymn Of Concern

"In The Hour Of Trial"                                       (Penitence)

In the hour of trial, Jesus plead for me;
Lest by base denial I depart from Thee;
When Thou seest me waver, with a look recall,
Nor for fear or favor suffer me to fall.

With forbidden pleasures would this vain world charm,
Or its sordid treasures spread to work me harm.
Bring to my remembrance sad Gethsemane,
Or, in darker semblance, cross-crowned Calvary. Amen.

## The Scripture Reading                    Luke 22:54-62

Then they seized him and led him away, bringing him into the high priest's house. Peter followed at a distance; and when they had kindled a fire in the middle of the courtyard and sat down together, Peter sat among them.

Then a maid, seeing him as he sat in the light and gazing at him, said, "This man also was with him." But he denied it, saying, "Woman, I do not know him." And a little later someone else saw him and said, "You also are one of them." But Peter said, "Man, I am not." And after an interval of about an hour still another insisted, saying, "Certainly this man was also with him; for he is a Galilean." But Peter said, "Man, I do not know what you are saying." And immediately, while he was still speaking, the cock crowed.

And the Lord turned and looked at Peter. And Peter remembered the word of the Lord, how he had said to him, "Before the cock crows today, you will deny me three times." And he went out, and wept bitterly.

## The Meditation

Peter was certain that Jesus would be able to overcome the evil forces that were opposing him. He had listened to him declare what lay ahead, but responded with, "No, no; that cannot be!" Jesus had unlimited power and Peter felt he would use it against his enemies. He really couldn't bring himself around to believing that death was near at hand.

The other disciples looked to Peter as the example of loyalty and devotion. He had been so near to Jesus in so many experiences, and he had declared that he was the long-promised Messiah. Now, suddenly, he was thrust into an unforeseen situation. Before he realized what was happening, he had uttered words of denial — not once, but three times. When he heard the cock crow, the words of Jesus came back to him and he realized the implication of what he had done. The one who had been a symbol of strength and loyalty to his Lord had, in a few short hours, become a symbol of weakness and denial.

How was it that Peter could use the same tongue to deny his Lord that he had earlier used to tell him of his devotion? He had actually done that which he had said that he would never do, in an effort to save his own skin. He was heartsick, but he could not retract the words that he had spoken.

The dawn had begun, with the soft rays of the early morning sun projecting a glimmer of light, but Peter seemed to be surrounded by darkness — the darkness of the forthcoming cross of his Master.

Who comes first in your life? Do you place Christ and his kingdom in first place, or do you really come first? Have you denied your faith, and your Lord, for your own personal gain? Are you willing to take a stand in support of your Savior, in return for what he has done for you? Will you support him with your loyalty and devotion, or will you deny him when the time of testing comes?

**The Prayer**

Father, sometimes we have failed You when You really needed a strong witness for your cause. Be merciful to us, and forgive us for being lukewarm in our loyalty. Guide us, that we might develop a rock-like faith within and express a stronger loyalty to You, through Christ. Amen.

*(The second candle is extinguished)*

## The Shadow Of Rejection

**The Anthem**

**The Scripture Reading**                                      Mark 15:6-14

Now at the feast he used to release for them any one prisoner for whom they asked. And among the rebels in prison, who had committed murder in the insurrection, there was a man called Barabbas. And the crowd came up and began to ask Pilate to do as he was wont to do for them. And he answered them, "Do you want me to release for you the King of the Jews?" For he perceived that it was out of envy that the chief priests had delivered him up. But the chief priests stirred up the crowd to have him release for them Barabbas instead.

And Pilate again said to them, "Then what shall I do with the man whom you call the King of the Jews?" And they cried out again, "Crucify him." And Pilate said to them, "Why, what evil has he done?" But they shouted all the more, "Crucify him."

**The Meditation**

What kind of crowd was it that asked for the release of Barabbas and the crucifixion of Jesus? What did they have against this teacher from Galilee? The people had been with him in large numbers earlier in the week — coming from Bethany, entering the city, going up to the Temple — but their reaction was now suddenly hostile. They had hailed him as their leader, and had listened to his teaching; how could they suddenly turn against him and request his death?

There were two groups of people in the crowd outside Pilate's chamber. There were those who had been emotionally stirred up, and perhaps bribed by some of the priests and elders; these were the ones who shouted, "Crucify him!" There were probably few, if any, of his followers in this group. But there was also a second group; this was the multitude who stood by and did nothing. Even though many of them believed that what was happening was wrong, they just went along with those who yelled the loudest. There were many followers in this group, but they let the mob spirit influence Pilate in making his decision.

While we would condemn those who wanted Jesus crucified, we must also be critical of those who failed to have the courage to stand up for their convictions. Let us never forget that public apathy is just as wrong as public hysteria. The influence of public opinion is very important to those in positions of political power. Christians have an obligation to stand up for that which is just and honest, especially where the rights of other people are involved.

Many of the people of the crowd became lost in the shadows of evil and trickery that morning. Before they realized it, they were "swallowed up" by the darkness of indifference and uttered not a word to support their Lord.

Do you join the crowd in shouting, "Crucify him," as you fail to take a stand for good in the face of evil? Do you crucify him anew as you see injustice around you and do nothing about it? Are you willing to stand up for your Christian convictions, even if it means standing alone and going against the will of the majority?

**The Prayer**

Forgive us for our silence and our apathy, Lord, and for failing to take a strong stand for You and your Church. Give us the courage we need to make an unfaltering testimony for You; help us witness to You and your truth by our words and our deeds, in your name. Amen.

*(The third candle is extinguished)*

### The Shadow Of Injustice

**The Hymn Of Suffering**

"O Sacred Head, Now Wounded"  (Passion Chorale)

O Sacred Head, now wounded,
With grief and shame weighed down,
Now scornfully surrounded
With thorns, Thine only crown;
How pale Thou art with anguish,
With sore abuse and scorn!
How does that visage languish
Which once was bright as morn!

What Thou, my Lord, hast suffered
Was all for sinners' gain;
Mine, mine was the transgression,
But Thine the deadly pain.

Lo, here I fall, my Savior!
'Tis I deserve Thy place;
Look on me with Thy favor,
Vouchsafe to me Thy grace. Amen.

**The Scripture Reading**　　　　　　　　Matthew 27:24-26

So when Pilate saw that he was gaining nothing, but rather that a riot was beginning, he took water and washed his hands before the crowd, saying, "I am innocent of this man's blood, see to it yourselves." And all the people answered, "His blood be on us and on our children."

Then he released for them Barabbas, and having scourged Jesus, delivered him to be crucified.

**The Meditation**

Pilate tried in every way to delay making a decision concerning Jesus. He sent him to Herod in the hope that he would take this problem off his hands. Pilate could not find Jesus in violation of any law, and believed that he was innocent of the charges that had been placed against him. However, he also realized the pressure of popular opinion; the people had to be satisfied with him as governor, or they would complain to Rome. He knew that he should release him, but he was afraid of what the consequences might be.

Pilate decided to play politics with the life of Jesus. He didn't want to feel any personal guilt from this decision, so he conceived the idea of letting the people decide. Perhaps he thought they would ask him to release Jesus, but he was mistaken. He failed to realize how the crowd had been stirred up by the clever priests and elders. He made the decision to follow the whims of the people — an act that was decisive and final. As soon as he had made it, he knew within his own mind that he had made the wrong one.

Here was a great opportunity for Pilate to have been known throughout history as the one who protected Jesus, but the shallowness of his conviction prevailed. Instead, we remember him for what he really was — a political ruler who was most concerned about saving his own neck.

Now the clouds of injustice invaded the city of Jerusalem, with heavy shadows of malice and hatred within, as they drove Jesus nearer to his cross — and death.

Are you aware of political leaders today who are like Pilate, who use any means they can to foster their own fortune and power? Do you help elect those who are less concerned about ethical standards and justice than they are about being popular and becoming re-elected? Do you support leaders who can reduce your taxes, even though the means may be questionable, or do you give your loyalty to those who stand for equality and righteousness?

## The Prayer

Lord, help us to remain firm in our Christian convictions. Grant us renewed spiritual strength, that we may not be easily swayed by those around us who do not follow your way or seek to do your will. Guide us each day with the power of your Spirit from within, as in the name of Jesus Christ we pray. Amen.

*(The fourth candle is extinguished)*

## The Shadow Of Torture

## The Hymn Of Penitence

"When I Survey The Wondrous Cross" (Hamburg)

When I survey the wondrous cross
On which the Prince of Glory died,
My richest gain I count but loss,
And pour contempt on all my pride.

Were the whole realm of nature mine,
That were a present far too small;
Love so amazing, so divine,
Demands my soul, my life, my all. Amen.

## The Scripture Reading          Mark 15:16-20

And the soldiers led him away inside the palace (that is, the praetorium); and they called together the whole battalion. And they clothed him in a purple cloak, and plaiting a crown of thorns they put it on him. And they began to salute him, "Hail, King of the Jews!" And they struck his head with a reed, and spat upon him, and they knelt down in homage to him. And when they had mocked him, they stripped him of the purple cloak, and put his own clothes on him. And they led him out to crucify him.

## The Meditation

The soldiers of Rome made sport of Jesus. They gave him a royal robe and hailed him as a king, in mockery. A crown was made from a thorn bush and placed upon his head in jest. Their sneers continued as they thrust in his hand a royal scepter in the form of a reed.

The legionnaires were cruel and callous within. They usually tortured those condemned to death before taking them to the place of crucifixion. It was their business to conquer the enemy and maintain order. As long as these two duties were fulfilled, few of their other actions were questioned. Since they were denied participating in some of the mad pleasures of the people, they found enjoyment in inflicting pain and misery upon those destined for Golgotha.

The torture borne by Jesus was not all physical in nature. While there was pain from the wounds in his head and body, the mental and emotional torment was even worse. The soldiers mocked him as a king and bowed before him as an insult, saying with a smirk — "Hail, King of the Jews." Jesus had endured the trick questions of the scribes and Pharisees; he had seen some of his followers dwindle away, but never before had he been forced to endure such humiliation.

The streets of the city seemed to be completely engulfed in shadows as Jesus carried his cross toward Golgotha. Most of those standing by looked at him through the morning light, but it was as though they were blinded by the darkness of bewilderment, for they did not realize what was happening before them.

Do you torture your Lord and Master by putting your personal pleasure in first place in your life? Do you insult him by claiming to be a follower of his, but actually disbelieve in him in your own heart? Do you wound him by the words you say against him, or by the words you fail to speak when he is depending upon you for a witness?

**The Prayer**

Savior, forgive us for the unnecessary torture that we may have inflicted upon You. Forgive us for those spiritual wounds we have made by our evil words and deeds. Pardon us if we have caused you to be crucified anew by our lack of loyalty and devotion. Grant us a renewed spirit within us, as in your name we pray. Amen.

*(The fifth candle is extinguished)*

### The Shadow Of Ridicule

**The Hymn Of Sorrow**

"Beneath The Cross Of Jesus" (St. Christopher)

Beneath the cross of Jesus I fain would take my stand —
The shadow of a mighty rock within a weary land;
A home within the wilderness, a rest upon the way,
From the burning of the noon-day heat, and the burden of the day.

Upon the cross of Jesus mine eyes at times can see
The very dying form of one who suffered there for me;
And from my stricken heart with tears two wonders I confess —
The wonders of redeeming love and my unworthiness. Amen.

**The Scripture Reading** Luke 23:39-43

One of the criminals who were hanged railed at him, saying, "Are you not the Christ? Save yourself and us!" But the other rebuked him, saying, "Do you not fear God, since you are under the same sentence of condemnation? And we indeed justly; for we are receiving the due reward of our deeds; but this man has done nothing wrong." And he said, "Jesus, remember me when you come in your kingly power." And he said to him, "Truly, I say to you, today, you will be with me in Paradise."

## The Meditation

As the two thieves hung upon their crosses, awaiting their death, they heard the voice of the third man hanging there. They heard him pray for the forgiveness of those who were jeering at him, for those who hated him, and for those who had nailed him there. They knew that their dying companion was not just an ordinary criminal; apparently they realized that this was Jesus, the one who claimed to be the Son of God. In spite of this, their attitudes toward Jesus and toward death were quite different. In fact, through their words we see that they represent two great classes of humanity.

The one thief had compassion as he was drawn near to Jesus through the suffering they were experiencing. He not only rebuked the other thief for his defiant attitude, but he also expressed his belief in Jesus. His confession was accepted by Jesus, who promised him the reward of eternal life.

The other thief was defiant and callous to the very end. The only life force he knew was that of power and might. He was only willing to believe in Jesus if he could show that he was able to triumph over his enemies with a display of supernatural power. He was concerned only about himself as he yelled, "Are you not the Christ? Save yourself and us!" He met his death damned by his own bitterness and selfishness.

With the scorn of the unrepentant thief, the darkness increased around the cross. This was most evident in the mind of Jesus as he realized that while some men would accept and follow him, there would be those who would reject him and have nothing to do with his kingdom.

Each one of us has a cross to bear, even though it may be different for each individual. How do you react to your cross? Does it bring you nearer to Christ, since you know that he suffered, too? Or, do you become bitter and turn your back on God, eliminating any means of help he might be able to give you?

### The Prayer

Father, speak to us in the midst of the difficult hours of life. Help us to lean upon You as we face adversity, illness, or difficulty, knowing that You will give us the faith sufficient to meet every need. Uplift us, as we carry our own crosses, knowing that the burden will not be nearly as heavy with your spiritual power undergirding us. We pray in Jesus' name. Amen.

*(The sixth candle is extinguished)*

### The Shadow Of Mockery

### The Scripture Reading                    Matthew 27:39-50

And those who passed by derided him, wagging their heads and saying, "You who would destroy the temple and build it in three days, save yourself! If you are the Son of God, come down from the cross." So also the chief priests, with the scribes and elders, mocked him, saying, "He saved others; he cannot save himself. He is the King of Israel; let him come down now from the cross, and we will believe in him. He trusts in God; let God deliver him now, if he desires him; for he said, "I am the Son of God."

Now from the sixth hour there was darkness over all the land until the ninth hour. And about the ninth hour Jesus cried with a loud voice, "Eli, Eli lama sabachthani?" that is "My God, my God, why hast thou forsaken me?" And some of the bystanders hearing it said, "This man is calling Elijah." And one of them at once ran and took a sponge, filled it with vinegar, and put it on a reed, and gave it to him to drink. But the others said, "Wait, let us see whether Elijah will come to save him." And Jesus cried again with a loud voice and yielded up his spirit.

### The Meditation

The religious leaders of Jerusalem were jealous of the power that Jesus possessed. They could not perform miracles and some of the people were beginning to doubt their authority. While many were not serious followers of Jesus, their number was large enough to cause great concern on the part of the scribes and priests.

Perhaps these leaders really wanted Jesus to come down from the cross and perform another miracle. However, one doubts whether they would have followed him even if he had done this. He had already done enough miracles, and answered sufficient questions, for them to have become followers if they wanted to do so. They really wanted to mock him, and in so doing hoped to belittle him before the crowd.

These leaders were shocked by the response of Jesus, which was complete silence. If they had expected a miracle, they should have realized that during his ministry he had only used miracles to help others, and not merely to demonstrate his power. If they had expected a verbal answer to their words, they were disappointed. The silence that followed seemed to indicate more than any words could have said. He well knew that his kingdom had to be built upon men who would follow him, not because of miracles or argumentation, but because of their faith in him as the very Son of God.

The shadows hung heavy over Golgotha, as dark clouds moved in from all directions. The three crosses were completely surrounded by darkness, but through it all something great was happening. The religious leaders, the soldiers, the curiosity seekers, and the mockers were spiritually blinded by the shadows around the cross. However, the followers who remained were privileged to be eye-witnesses to the power of Almighty God revealing the greatness of his love for all humankind.

Have you allowed yourself to be spiritually blinded to what the power of God can do for you? As a leader in his Church, do you live and act in the spirit of Christ, or in the spirit of the scribes and priests? Have you permitted the shadows of disbelief to close your eyes and cover your ears to Jesus Christ and the greatness of his message of love and salvation?

### The Prayer

Lord, forgive us when we have permitted the types of shadows that surrounded the cross of Jesus to keep us from realizing your spiritual presence in our lives. Might we never forget that he gave his life upon that cross for our sins, and for the sins of all humankind. Inspire us to spread the message of your love, come to us through Jesus Christ, our Lord and Savior. Amen.

*(The seventh candle is extinguished)*

**The Hymn Of Victory**

"In The Cross Of Christ I Glory" (Rathbun)

In the cross of Christ I glory,
Towering o'er the wrecks of time:
All the light of sacred story
Gathers round its head sublime.

When the woes of life o'ertake me,
Hopes deceive and fears annoy,
Never shall the cross forsake me:
Lo! It glows with peace and joy. Amen.

**The Benediction**

**The Postlude**

### ALTERNATE ENDING

### The Shadow Of The Tomb

*(Service continues in semi-darkened sanctuary)*

**The Scripture Reading** Luke 23:50-56

**The Brief Meditation**

We have just witnessed, in a spiritual manner, the way in which shadows came toward the cross of Jesus from every direction. We have visualized how these shadows accumulated and produced the blackest clouds that ever darkened the world. But we know that through this experience we have received pardon and forgiveness for our sins. Let this service ever be a sacred reminder of the gift of God's love for all of us.

But let us also depart from this place realizing that death was not the end. Even though they laid his body in a tomb, there was none strong enough to contain him. We rejoice in the fact that, through his death upon the cross, Jesus became the Christ, the Savior of humankind, and revealed himself completely as the Son of God. After three days he defied death, he repelled darkness, and turned tragedy into triumph. He emerged from the shadows of the tomb to become the light of the world!

*(An eighth candle is lighted and placed upon the altar. The absence of light has symbolized the three days spent by Christ in the tomb. This candle is lighted in anticipation of the light of Easter morning; it remains lighted as the worshipers leave the service.)*

**The Hymn Of Dedication**

"O Love That Wilt Not Let Me Go" (St. Margaret)

O Love that wilt not let me go,
I rest my weary soul in Thee;
I give Thee back the life I owe,
That in Thine ocean depths its flow
May richer, fuller be.

O cross that liftest up my head,
I dare not ask to fly from thee;
I lay in dust life's glory dead,
And from the ground there blossoms red
Life that shall endless be. Amen.

**The Prayer Of Dedication**

**The Benediction**

**The Postlude**